Cooking for Muggles

The Harry Potter Cookbook

Harry Potter Recipes with Desserts, Snacks and Drinks
Inspired by Harry Potter Food

By
Martha Stephenson

Copyright 2016 Martha Stephenson

License Notes

No part of this Book can be reproduced in any form or by any means including print, electronic, scanning or photocopying unless prior permission is granted by the author.

All ideas, suggestions and guidelines mentioned here are written for informative purposes. While the author has taken every possible step to ensure accuracy, all readers are advised to follow information at their own risk. The author cannot be held responsible for personal and/or commercial damages in case of misinterpreting and misunderstanding any part of this Book

Table of Contents

Introduction 5
Chapter 1 – Harry Potter Cake and Cake Pop Recipes 6
    Rock Cakes 7
    Golden Snitch Cake Pops 10
    Cauldron Cakes 13
    Butterbeer Cupcakes 15
    Hagrid's Birthday Cake for Harry 19
Chapter 2 – Harry Potter Dessert Recipes 23
    Treacle Tart 24
    Pumpkin Pasties 27
    Luna's Pudding 30
    Mrs. Weasley's Homemade Fudge 33
Chapter 3 – Harry Potter Snack Recipes 35
    Acid Pops 36
    Licorice Wands 38
    Cockroach Clusters 40
    Chocolate Frogs 42
    Ollivander's Wands 44
    Weasleys' Dragon Roasted Nuts 46

- Chapter 4 – Harry Potter Drink Recipes 48
  - Pumpkin Juice 49
  - Polyjuice Potion Punch 51
  - Dragon's Blood Punch 53
  - Goblet of Fire (Alcoholic) 55
- Chapter 5 – Butterbeer Recipes 57
  - Traditional Butterbeer 58
  - Butterbeer for Adults 60
  - Simple Butterbeer 62
  - Frozen Butterbeer 64
  - Butterbeer Latte 66
  - Vegan Butterbeer 68
- Conclusion 70
- About the Author 71
- Author's Afterthoughts 73

Introduction

I want to thank you and congratulate you for downloading the book, "Cooking for Muggles: The Harry Potter Cookbook with Desserts, Snacks and Drinks Inspired by Harry Potter Food".

You may think that just because you're a muggle that you cannot make the delicious desserts, snacks and drinks found in the magical world of Harry Potter. And you couldn't be further from the truth. In fact, this Harry Potter cookbook proves that you don't have to be a witch or a wizard, or have any magic powers at all, to make the many delicious treats found throughout the Harry Potter series of books and movies. The recipes found within this cookbook lets you bring a little bit of magic to your kitchen table.

Thanks again for downloading this book, I hope you enjoy it! Now what are you waiting for? Get started reading Chapter 1 now!

Chapter 1 – Harry Potter Cake and Cake Pop Recipes

Rock Cakes

Mrs. Weasley's famous rock cakes are not named because they are hard liken rocks, which they're not, but because they have a rock-like shape. These delicious cakes are similar to scones and feature a yummy spice flavor that is perfect for the fall and winter seasons.

Serving: 12 to 16 cakes

Total Time: 25 to 30 minutes

Ingredients:

- 4 cups flour, self-raising
- 1 cup butter, unsalted
- ½ teaspoon salt, kosher
- 2 teaspoon pumpkin pie spice
- 1 cup currants, dried
- 1 cup + extra sugar, granulated
- 4 large eggs, room temperature
- ½ cup milk, whole

Directions:

Step 1: Preheat oven to 400-degrees. Lightly grease the bottom of a cookie sheet. Set to the side for the moment.

Step 2: In a mixing bowl, sift the flour, pumpkin pie spice and salt together. Use your hands to knead the softened butter into the flour mixture. Continue kneading until the mixture has large crumbs.

Step 3: Add the dried currants and the 1 cup of granulated sugar into the mixture. Stir until well mixed.

Step 4: In a small bowl, whisk the milk and egg together until well combined. Stir this mixture into the flour mixture until just combined.

Step 5: Drop spoonful dollops of the dough onto the prepared cookie sheet from Step 1. Make sure to leave about 1 ½-inch in between each cookie.

Step 6: Sprinkle a bit of granulated sugar over each dollop of cookie dough.

Step 7: Place the cookie dough into the preheated oven and bake for 15 minutes.

Step 8: Remove the cookie sheet from the oven and transfer the rock cakes to a cooling rack. Let the rock cakes cool before serving.

Golden Snitch Cake Pops

As any Potterhead knows, the golden snitch is one of the most important aspects of Quidditch. In order for the game to end, the Seeker has to catch the snitch. And you can make your own edible version with this cake pop recipe, which can be altered by changing the type of cake and frosting used.

Total Time: 70 to 80 minutes

Ingredients:

- 1 box yellow cake mix
- 3 large eggs
- ¼ cup vegetable oil
- 1 can cream cheese frosting
- 1 bag yellow candy melts
- Lollipop sticks
- Styrofoam block
- Edible gold dust or edible gold spray

Directions:

Step 1: Bake the cake according to the directions on the back of the package. For best results, bake the cake in a 9x13-inch baking pan. Once the cake is done, remove it from the oven and set to the side to cool.

Step 2: Once the cake is cooled, use a fork to mash it up. No need to transfer the cake into a mixing bowl, just mash it up right in the baking pan.

Step 3: Add ½ cup of the frosting into the crumbled up cake and mix until well combined.

Step 4: Use your hands to roll the mixture into balls measuring about an inch in diameter. Place the balls on a cookie sheet covered with parchment paper and let firm up in the freezer for about 15 minutes.

Step 5: Following the melting instructions on the package, melt the yellow candy melts in a microwave-safe bowl.

Step 6: Dip the end of a lollipop stick in the melted yellow melts. Insert the yellow-covered part of the stick in a cake ball. Continue in this manner until all cake balls have a lollipop stick inserted into them.

Step 7: While holding the cake ball its stick, dip the cake ball into the melted chocolate, swirling it until completely covered. Stick the covered cake balls into the Styrofoam block, right side up. Continue in this manner until all the cake balls have been coated.

Step 8: Let the melted chocolate harden on the cake balls before spraying them with edible gold spray or gold dust.

Tips: For even more realism, add wings to each snitch. This can be done by making edible wings out of white chocolate and a leaf mold or white fondant.

Cauldron Cakes

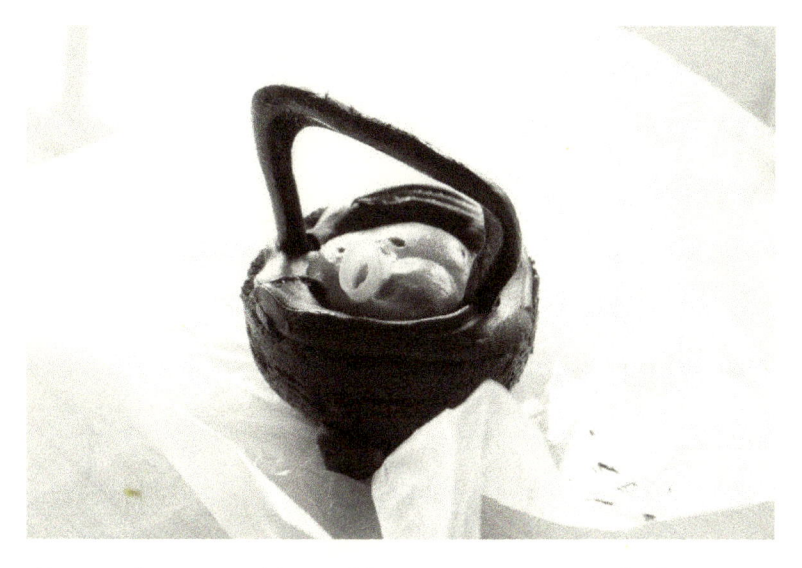

These cakes resemble cauldrons, a common tool of wizards, and feature an oozing middle.

Serving: 4

Total Time: 55 to 60 minutes

Cake Ingredients:

- 1 cup flour, self-raising
- 2 tablespoons unsweetened cocoa powder
- 1 ¼ cup packed brown sugar
- 1 teaspoon vanilla
- ¼ cup unsalted butter, melted
- ½ cup whole milk
- 1 large egg, room temperature and lightly beaten

Sauce Ingredients:

- 2 tablespoons unsweetened cocoa powder
- 1 cup packed brown sugar
- 1 ¼ cups boiling water
- 4 oven-proof baking containers

Directions:

Step 1: Preheat your oven to 350-degrees.

Step 2: Sift the flour, brown sugar and cocoa together in a mixing bowl. Add the butter, vanilla, egg and milk, and stir until just combined. Avoid overmixing as this will make the cake tough.

Step 3: Spoon the mixture into the 4 baking containers, making sure you leave room at the top for the sauce and for the cakes to rise. Set to the side while you make the sauce.

Step 4: Make the sauce by mixing the cocoa and brown sugar. Spoon this dry mixture over top each of the 4 cakes. Set the cakes on a baking sheet.

Step 5: Pour the water overtop the dry sauce mixture. Place the cakes in the preheated oven and bake for about 40 minutes.

Butterbeer Cupcakes

This recipe takes the delicious flavor of butterbeer and turns it into a cupcake!

Serving: 18 to 20

Total Time: 60 to 65 minutes

Cupcake Ingredients:

- 2 cups flour, all-purpose
- 1 cup brown sugar, packed
- 1 teaspoon baking powder
- 1 teaspoon baking soda
- ½ teaspoon salt
- ½ cup oil, vegetable or canola
- 3 large eggs, room temperature
- 1 teaspoon vanilla extract
- 1 teaspoon butter extract

- ½ cup buttermilk
- ½ cup cream soda
- 1 cup toffee bits

Sauce Ingredients:

- ½ cup heavy cream
- ¾ cup butterscotch chips

Frosting Ingredients:

- 2 cups heavy cream
- ½ cup powdered sugar
- 1/3 cup butterscotch pudding mix, instant
- 3 teaspoon butter extract
- Sprinkles (optional)

Directions:

Step 1: Turn the oven to 350-degrees and let preheat. Prepare a cupcake pan by lining it with cupcake liners. Set to the side for the moment.

Step 2: In a mixing bowl, sift the flour, baking powder, baking soda, salt and sugar together.

Step 3: Using a mixer with a whisk attachment, mix the buttermilk, eggs, extracts and oil together until combined. Gradually beat in the mixture from Step 2, followed by the cream soda. Continue to mix until the ingredients are smooth.

Step 4: Fold the toffee bits by hand into the mixture.

Step 5: Add about ¼ cup of the batter into each of the liner-lined cupcake tin. Place the tin in the preheated oven and bake for 20 to 22 minutes. Continue in this manner until you have made all the cupcakes.

Step 6: While the cupcakes are baking, make the sauce by warming the cream on the stove over medium heat. Place the butterscotch chips in a metal bowl and set to the side for the moment.

Step 7: Continue to heat the cream until it starts to simmer. Once simmering, pour it over the butterscotch chips and let sit for a few minutes before whisking until smooth. Set the bowl in the fridge for about 25 minutes to thicken the sauce.

Step 8: Make the frosting by mixing all the frosting ingredients together until the mixture is fluffy and light. Transfer the frosting into a decorating bag with the desired tip attached. If you don't have a decorating bag, you can simply spread the frosting on the cupcakes using a butter knife.

Step 9: Spread the sauce from Step 7 on a piece of wax paper. Take the cooled cupcakes and dip just the tops of them in the sauce. Set the cupcakes to the side for 15 to 20 minutes.

Step 10: Place each cupcake in a second cupcake liner to cover up the liner that the cupcake was baked in. This step isn't required but it does make the cupcakes look more professional and nicer.

Step 11: Frost each cupcake as desired and top with sprinkles if desired.

Hagrid's Birthday Cake for Harry

On Harry's 11th birthday, Hagrid made Harry a chocolate birthday cake covered in pink frosting and decorated with "Happee Birthdae Harry" in green lettering. While Hagrid may not be the best of bakers, you does mean well. This version of that cake is much better tasting and can be altered to fit the type of cake you want.

Serving: 8 to 10

Total Time: 55 to 65 minutes

Cake Ingredients:

- 1 ¼ cup + 2 tablespoons all-purpose flour
- 1 ½ cup granulated sugar
- ½ cup + 2 tablespoons unsweetened cocoa powder
- 1 1/8 teaspoon baking powder
- 1 1/8 teaspoon baking soda
- ¾ teaspoon salt
- 1 large egg
- 1 large yolk
- ¾ cup whole milk
- ¼ cup + 2 tablespoons oil, vegetable or canola
- 1 ½ teaspoon vanilla
- ¾ cup water, boiling

Frosting Ingredients:

- 3 tablespoons unsalted butter, at room temperature
- 1/6 cup whole milk
- 2 cups powdered sugar
- ½ teaspoon vanilla
- Food coloring, red and green

Directions:

Step 1: Preheat the oven to 350-degrees. Spray the bottom and sides of a 12 x 9-inch baking sheet with non-stick spray. Set to the side for the moment.

Step 2: Sift the flour, sugar, baking powder, baking soda, salt and cocoa powder together. Add the egg and the egg yolk and stir until combined.

Step 3: Stir in the oil, milk and vanilla. Once the mixture is well combined, add the boiling water and stir until just combined. Spread the mixture into the prepared baking sheet from Step 1.

Step 4: Bake the cake in the preheated oven for about 30 minutes. Once a toothpick, when inserted in the middle, comes out clean, remove the cake from the oven and let cool.

Step 5: Carefully flip the cooled cake out of the baking sheet and onto a flat surface.

Step 6: While the cake is cooling, make the frosting by whisking the butter, sugar, milk and vanilla together. Remove a bit of the frosting and set to the side in a small bowl for the moment.

Step 7: Add the red food coloring, one drop at a time, to the larger amount of frosting, making sure to stir until the food coloring is mixed throughout the frosting. Continue adding the food coloring until you get the desired ugly pink color. Spread the pink frosting over the top and sides of the cooled cake.

Step 8: Add the green food coloring, one drop at a time, to the little bit of frosting that you set to the side. Continue mixing in the food coloring until you achieve the desired green color.

Step 9: Transfer the green frosting into a decorating page fitted with a writing tip. Write the desired message, such as "Happee Birthdae Harry" on the cake with the green frosting.

Chapter 2 – Harry Potter Dessert Recipes

Treacle Tart

This traditional English dessert is one of Harry Potter's favorite, and Ron uses it to try to entice Hermione to eat while naming all the goodies made by the Hogwart's house elves.

Serving:

Total Time: 80 to 85 minutes

Tart Base Ingredients:

- 1 cup flour, all-purpose
- ¾ stick unsalted butter, softened
- Pinch table salt
- 2 ½ tablespoons cold water

Filling Ingredients:

- ¼ stick unsalted butter, softened
- Juice from half a lemon
- Zest from half a lemon
- 1 teaspoon rosemary, chopped finely
- 2/3 cup + 1 tablespoon golden syrup
- 1 cup + ¼ cup breadcrumbs
- 1 large egg, room temperature
- 2/3 cup almond meal

Directions:

Step 1: Preheat oven to 375-degrees. Lightly grease a 9 1/2-inch pie or tart tin. Set to the side for the moment.

Step 2: Start making the base of the tart by kneading the softened butter into the flour. Continue to knead until the mixture has the consistency of sand. Add a little bit of ice water to the mixture and continue to knead until the gritty mixture has a soft dough like texture.

Step 3: Evenly press the dough into the prepared pie or tart tin, making sure to press it into the bottom and along the sides. Bake the dough in the preheated oven for about 30 minutes. You want the dough to be cooked through and have a light golden color.

Step 4: Start making the filling by melting the butter in a saucepan over low heat. When the butter begins to foam, stir in the lemon juice, lemon zest, rosemary, golden syrup, breadcrumbs and almond meal. Once the mixture is well combined remove it from heat and let cool for a bit.

Step 5: Remove the base of the tart from the oven and set to the side to cool for a few minutes.

Step 6: Whisk the egg into the filling mixture from Step 4. Pour the filling mixture directly into the base of the tart. Put the tart back in the oven and bake for about 20 minutes.

Step 7: Once the tart is done, set but middle still jiggles slightly, remove it from the oven and let cool for 20 or more minutes before serving.

Pumpkin Pasties

Serving: 4

Total Time:

Ingredients:

- 1 pound pumpkin
- 4 tablespoons unsalted butter
- 1 garlic clove, minced
- ½ cup white cheddar cheese, shredded
- Salt, to taste
- Ground black pepper, to taste
- 1 package pie crust, refrigerated
- All-purpose flour, for dusting
- Heavy cream, for brushing

Directions:

Step 1: Preheat the oven to 400-degrees.

Step 2: Cut the pumpkin in half and discard the seeds and pulp. Place the sliced pumpkin on a baking sheet and roast in the oven until the flesh is warm and tender. Scoop the tender flesh out of the pumpkin shell and place in a large mixing bowl.

Step 3: Use a potato masher to mash the pumpkin with the butter. You want the mixture to resemble the same consistency as mashed potatoes. Add the minced garlic and cheese and mash until well combined. Season the mixture with salt and pepper. Set to the side for the moment.

Step 4: Lightly dust a flat surface with the all-purpose flour. Carefully roll the refrigerated pie crust onto the surface. The pie crust should be rolled to about 1/8-inch thickness.

Step 5: Using a 7-inch circle cookie cutter, cut the pie crust into 4 circles.

Step 6: Spoon about ½ cup of the mixture from Step 2 into the center of each one of the pie crust circles. Carefully fold the crust over the pumpkin filling. You should be left with a half-moon shape pastry. Use a fork to press the ends of the dough crust to seal the pastry.

Step 7: Cut 3 small slices on the top of each pastry. These small slices will act as ventilation. Place the pastries to a parchment paper-covered baking sheet. Brush each pastry lightly with heavy cream.

Step 8: Place the pastries in the preheated oven and bake for about 30 minutes. The pastries should have a nice golden brown color.

Step 9: Let the pumpkin pastries cool for about 5 minutes before serving.

Luna's Pudding

Luna Lovegood may be the most unusual students ever to attend Hogwarts. This eccentric, intelligent and caring girl has a taste for pudding and this delicious recipe perfectly combines the weirdness of the character with a classical taste.

Serving: 4 to 8

Total Time: 30 to 35 minutes + 60 minutes to chill

Pudding Base Ingredients:

- 10 tablespoons granulated sugar
- ½ teaspoon salt
- 5 tablespoons cornstarch
- 5 cups milk, low-fat
- 3 tablespoons unsalted butter, softened
- 4 large egg yolks, lightly beaten
- 1 ½ tablespoons vanilla

Whipped Cream Ingredients:

- ¼ cup granulated sugar
- 1 ½ cups heavy whipping cream
- 2 teaspoon vanilla extract
- Toppings and Extras
- 2 cups blueberries, diced
- 2 cups strawberries, destemmed and diced
- 1 pound cake, cubed into bite-sized pieces
- Food coloring, pink
- Edible glitter

Directions:

Step 1: Pour the milk, cornstarch, sugar and salt into a saucepan. Set the saucepan on the stove over medium heat and whisk while you allow the mixture to simmer. Once the mixture has thickened a little, remove from heat and whisk in the egg yolks.

Step 2: Whisk in the vanilla and butter until the mixture is smooth and thoroughly combined. Set the pudding to the side for the moment to cool.

Step 3: Make the whipped cream by beating the heavy cream, vanilla and sugar together until peaks begin to form. Set the whipped cream to the side for the moment.

Step 4: Transfer the pudding from Step 2 into a bowl. Stir in two to three drops of the pink food coloring until you achieve the desired pretty pink color. Add the strawberries and stir until well combined.

Step 5: Scoop about half of the pudding mixture out of the bowl and into a trifle dish. Spread the pudding evenly in the dish. Layer about ½ of the pound cake over the pudding layer, followed by half of the whipped cream.

Step 6: Spread the remaining pudding mixture overtop the whipped cream. Layer the remaining pound cake, followed by the remaining whipped cream.

Step 7: Top with the blueberries and edible glitter before allowing the pudding to cool in the fridge for at least 60 minutes.

Mrs. Weasley's Homemade Fudge

On Christmas of 1991, Harry wasn't expecting to receive any presents but when he woke that morning he was pleasantly surprise to find more than a few gifts. One of them being Mrs. Weasley's homemade fudge.

Serving: 9 to 12

Total Time: 2 hours 30 minutes

Ingredients:

- 2 cups sugar, granulated
- ¼ cup cocoa powder, unsweetened
- ½ cup light corn syrup
- ½ cup chocolate, finally chopped

- ½ teaspoon salt
- 2 tablespoons unsalted butter, softened
- 1 cup half-and-half
- Candy thermometer

Directions:

Step 1: Line the bottom of an 8x8-inch baking sheet with parchment paper. Lightly grease the parchment paper. Set the baking sheet to the side for the moment.

Step 2: Place the sugar, cocoa powder, salt, chocolate, corn syrup and half-and-half into a pot. Set the pot on the stove over medium heat. Stir the ingredients together and let them come to a simmer. Continue to stir until the mixture reaches a temperature of 235-degrees.

Step 3: Remove the pot from the heat and let it cool down to 110-degrees. Once the mixture reaches this temperature, start stirring and continue to stir until it begins to lose its sheen.

Step 4: Carefully pour the mixture into the prepared pan from Step 1, making sure to smooth it out evenly.

Step 5: Set the fudge to the side and let cool for 2 or more hours. Once the fudge has set, cut it into squares and serve.

Chapter 3 – Harry Potter Snack Recipes

Acid Pops

Available at the Honeydukes sweetshop, acid pops are a practical joke treat that can burn a nasty hole in your tongue, which Ron found out when he was seven years old. This easy-to-recreate recipe uses premade lollipops for a quick Harry Potter-inspired treat!

Serving: 12

Total Time: 30 to 35 minutes

Ingredients:

- 12 sour lollipops
- 4 packages pop rocks
- ¼ cup raw honey
- Wax paper

Directions:

Step 1: Cover a cookie sheet with wax paper and set to the side for the moment.

Step 2: Remove and discard the wrapper from all the lollipops. Pour the pop rocks into a small bowl.

Step 3: Put the honey in a microwave-safe bowl. Place in the microwave and heat for about 30 seconds.

Step 4: Dip a lollipop in the warm honey making sure they are evenly coated. Roll the honey-coated lollipop in the pop rocks and set on the wax paper-covered cookie sheet from Step 1 to dry. Continue in this manner until you have coated and covered all the lollipops in honey and pop rocks.

Step 5: Serve the acid pops as soon as possible after drying.

Licorice Wands

No wizard is complete without their wand! While this wand recipe isn't the only one in this book, it is the only one that used licorice as the base of the wand.

Serving: 24 wands

Total Time: 10 to 15 minutes + 1 hour to firm

Ingredients:

- 6 ounces white chocolate melting chips
- 24 licorice twists
- Multi-colored sprinkles

Directions:

Step 1: Line the bottom of a baking sheet with wax paper. Set to the side for the moment.

Step 2: Pour the sprinkles into a shallow bowl.

Step 3: Following the directions on the back of the package, melt the white chocolate in a microwave-safe bowl. Transfer the melted chocolate into a tall, thin glass (this will make dipping the licorice easier).

Step 4: Dip about 1/3 of the licorice into the melted chocolate. Roll the chocolate-covered part of the licorice into the sprinkles until covered. Set on the prepared baking sheet from Step 1. Continue in this manner until all licorice twists have been turned into wands.

Step 5: Let the wands firm for about an hour before serving.

Cockroach Clusters

Found in Honeydukes sweetshop, these trick treats are made of cockroaches but shaped to look like peanuts. Ron thought about trying to fool Fred with these seemingly innocent-looking treats. This recipe forgoes the insects and instead uses dry noodles.

Serving: 12 cockroach clusters

Total Time: 15 minutes to prepare + 1 hour or more to firm

Ingredients:

- ¼ cup butterscotch chips
- ½ cup milk chocolate chips
- 1 ½ cup chow mein noodles, dry

Directions:

Step 1: Line the bottom of a baking sheet with wax paper. Set to the side for the moment.

Step 2: Melt the butterscotch chips and the milk chocolate chips together in a double boiler. Make sure to stir constantly throughout this process to prevent burning.

Step 3: Once the butterscotch and chocolate have melted and are smooth, remove them from heat.

Step 4: Add the dry noodles and stir until well mixed and coated. Drop the mixture by the spoonful onto the prepared baking sheet from Step 1.

Step 5: Let the clusters firm up. For faster firming, place the clusters in the fridge for 20 or so minutes.

Chocolate Frogs

Chocolate frogs are a frog-shaped confection that are popular throughout the wizarding world. These chocolate goodies are sold with collectible cards that feature famous witches and wizards. What's even better is that this recipe requires only 1 actual ingredient; chocolate! If, however, you want something more elaborate, you can add filling, such as marshmallow or peanut butter, to the frogs.

Serving: 12 frogs

Total Time: 20 to 30 minutes

Ingredients:

- 1 pound melting chocolate
- Frog mold

Directions:

Step 1: Use a double boiler to melt the chocolate, making sure to stir constantly to prevent the chocolate from burning.

Step 2: Remove the chocolate from heat and carefully pour into the frog-shape mold.

Step 3: Place the frog mold in the freezer and let harden for about 10 minutes. Carefully pop the firm chocolate out of the mold.

Step 4: Continue in this manner until you have used all the chocolate.

Ollivander's Wands

Garrick Ollivander was the owner of Ollivanders Wand Shop located in Diagon Alley. He was considered the greatest wandmaker ever and wizards all over the world would purchase their wands from him. This recipe is essentially chocolate covered pretzels and can be altered by using any flavor of chocolate, such as white, dark or mint.

Serving: 12 pretzel wands

Total Time: 15 minutes + 60 minutes to firm

Ingredients:

- 8 ounces melting milk chocolate
- 12 pretzel wands
- Sprinkles

Directions:

Step 1: Dump the sprinkles in a shallow dish and set to the side for the moment. Cover a baking sheet with parchment paper and set to the side for the moment.

Step 2: Melt the chocolate as directed on the packaging. This can generally be done either in the microwave or in a double boiler.

Step 3: Transfer the melted chocolate into a tall glass. This will make dipping the pretzel rods a bit easier.

Step 4: Dip about ½ to ¾ of the pretzel rod into the melted chocolate, making sure the pretzel is completely covered.

Step 5: Dip the tip of the chocolate-covered pretzel in the sprinkles. Lay the pretzel wand on the prepared baking sheet and let the chocolate firm before serving.

Weasleys' Dragon Roasted Nuts

Found in a coin operated machine in Diagon Alley, these delicious chestnuts where pleasantly roasted by miniature dragons.

Serving: 4

Total Time: 60 to 65 minutes

Ingredients:

- 1/2 teaspoon cayenne pepper
- ½ teaspoon cumin
- 12 teaspoon cinnamon
- 3 tablespoons brown sugar, packed
- ¼ teaspoon chili powder
- ½ teaspoon sea or table salt
- 1 cup almonds

- 1 large egg white, room temperature

Directions:

Step 1: Preheat the oven to 250-degrees. Prepare a baking sheet by lining it with parchment paper. Set to the side for the moment.

Step 2: Mix the cayenne pepper, cumin, cinnamon, brown sugar, chili powder and salt together until well combined.

Step 3: In a separate bowl, whisk the egg white for a few seconds. Place the almonds in the whisked egg whites and stir until the nuts are thoroughly covered.

Step 4: Transfer the egg white coated almonds into the bowl with the spices from Step 2. Toss to thoroughly coat the almonds.

Step 5: Spread the coated almonds evenly along the bottom of the prepared baking sheet from Step 1.

Step 6: Place the almonds in the preheated oven and bake for about 50 minutes. Remove the almonds from the oven and let cool on the baking sheet before serving.

Chapter 4 – Harry Potter Drink Recipes

(Alcoholic and Non Alcoholic)

Pumpkin Juice

In the wizarding world, pumpkin juice is one of the most popular beverages, especially with the students. It can be consumed on any occasion throughout the day. Pumpkin juice is often thought of as the magical cousin to the muggle's orange juice.

Serving: 4

Total Time: 10 to 15 minutes

Ingredients:

- 1 pumpkin, destemmed and seeded
- 2 red apples, destemmed and cored
- 2 lemon
- 2-inch piece ginger root, skinned
- Ice cubes (optional)

Directions:

Step 1: Cut the pumpkin, apple and lemon into small cubes that can fit into your juicer.

Step 2: Place all 4 ingredients into your juicer and, following the instructions for your specific type of juicer, juice the ingredients.

Step 3: Remove and discard the solids left over and strain the remaining juice through a sieve.

Step 4: Add some ice cubes to the glasses if desired. Pour the pumpkin juice into the glasses and serve.

Polyjuice Potion Punch

In the world of Harry Potter, polyjuice potion is a complex concoction that gives the drinker the ability to turn into someone else. While this punch recipe is delicious and looks magical, it doesn't have the same effects as the "real" polyjuice potion.

Serving: 10 to 20

Total Time: 10 to 15 minutes

Ingredients:

- ½ gallon lime sherbet
- 2 liters lemon and lime soft drink (such as Sprite)
- Food coloring, neon green
- Punch bowl

Directions:

Step 1: Open the sherbet carton by cutting the sides of the container so you can easily slide the sherbet into a punch bowl.

Step 2: Pour the 2 liters of soft drink slowly into the punch bowl and over the sherbet.

Step 3: Add a few drops of the neon green food coloring, making sure to stir after each addition. Continue to add the food coloring until you achieve the desired color.

Step 4: Serve the punch immediately or as soon as possible.

Dragon's Blood Punch

Dragon's blood has various uses in the world of Harry Potter. Albus Dumbledore discovered 12 uses for this expensive ingredient.

Serving: 20 to 25

Total Time: 5 to 8 minutes

Ingredients:

- 46-ounces red punch
- 48-ounces cranberry juice
- 46-ounces apple juice
- 2 liters ginger ale
- Ice cubes

Directions:

Step 1: Place the red punch, cranberry juice, apple juice and ginger ale into a large punch bowl. Slowly stir the mixture for a few seconds.

Step 2: Add some ice cubes and serve with a ladle.

Tips: You can make an alcoholic version of this punch by adding ½ cup of orange liqueur and 4 cups of berry vodka.

Goblet of Fire (Alcoholic)

The goblet of fire is a vital part of the Triwizard Tournament. The students place their name in the goblet. The goblet chooses which student by dramatically spitting their name out of the goblet.

Serving: 1

Total Time: 5 to 10 minutes

Ingredients:

- 3 ounces lemonade
- 1 ounce blue curacao
- 1 ounce vodka
- Splash rum, 151 proof
- Pinch ground cinnamon
- Goblet-style glass

Directions:

Step 1: Pour the lemonade, blue curacao and vodka into the glass.

Step 2: Add a splash of the rum and light the mixture on fire.

Tips: To make the drink spark, drop a pinch of the ground cinnamon into the flames. Make sure to blow out the flames before drinking this beverage.

Chapter 5 – Butterbeer Recipes

Traditional Butterbeer

Out of all the butterbeer recipes I have tried, this one tastes the closet to the beverage found at Universal's Wizarding World of Harry Potter.

Serving: 1

Total Time: 10 minutes

Base Ingredients:

- Cream Soda, chilled
- 2 teaspoon butterscotch syrup (such as sundae topping)

Topping Ingredients:

- ½ cup whipping heavy cream
- 1 teaspoon Jello mix, butterscotch-flavored
- ¼ cup powdered sugar

Directions:

Step 1: Place a mug in the freezer and let chill until ready to use.

Step 2: Place the heavy whipping cream, Jello mix and powdered sugar into a blender. Blend the mixture until the mixture is smooth and has the consistency similar of whipped cream. Set to the side for the moment.

Step 3: Remove the chilled mug from the freezer and fill it with the chilled cream soda. Make sure you leave a little bit of room for the topping.

Step 4: Stir in 2 teaspoons of the butterscotch syrup until well combined. Top the beverage with the whipped topping from Step 2 and enjoy.

Butterbeer for Adults

If you know the world of Harry Potter, then you know what butterbeer is. And this recipe contains actual beer to make a delicious, magical adult beverage. While this recipe recommends serving the beverage hot, it also includes instructions on making cold butterbeer for adults.

Serving: 2 large mugs

Total Time: 25 to 35 minutes

Ingredients:

- 24 ounces pumpkin ale
- 6 to 8 tablespoons butterscotch sauce

Directions:

Step 1: Whisk the beer and the butterscotch sauce together in a saucepan large enough to accommodate the ingredients. Place the pan on the stove and, while whisking occasionally, bring the mixture to just a boil. Remove the pan from the stove and serve immediately in large mugs.

Tip: If you want cold butterbeer, pour the ale into a blender and blend. While the ale is blending, gradually pour in the butterscotch sauce and continue to blend until combined. Try not to over blend the mixture as this will cause the ale to flatten. Divide the cold butterbeer between large mugs.

Simple Butterbeer

This butterbeer recipe is probably one of the simplest ones out there but still tastes good.

Serving: 1

Total Time: 5 minutes

Ingredients:

- 1 dollop heavy whipping cream
- 1 teaspoon butterscotch syrup
- Cream soda, chilled
- 1 teaspoon caramel syrup

Directions:

Step 1: In a small bowl, beat the whipping cream with the butterscotch syrup until frothy and light. Set to the side for the moment.

Step 2: Pour the cream soda into a mug. Stir in the caramel syrup until well mixed.

Step 3: Place the frothy topping from Step 1 on top and severe immediately.

Frozen Butterbeer

This recipe takes the delicious butterbeer flavor and turns it into more of a milkshake-like drink, making it perfect for those hot summer days.

Serving: 1

Total Time: 5 to 10 minutes

Ingredients:

- 2 scoops ice cream, vanilla
- 2 cup ice cubes, crushed
- 1 to 2 cups cream soda
- 3 tablespoons + extra butterscotch sauce
- Whipped cream

Directions:

Step 1: Blend the ice cubes, 1 cup of cream soda and ice cubes together in a blender. If necessary, add another cup of cream soda to thin the consistency of the drink.

Step 2: Add the butterscotch sauce and blend until well combined.

Step 3: Transfer the mixture into a mug. Top with some whipped cream and drizzle with a bit more of the butterscotch cause. Enjoy immediately.

Butterbeer Latte

If you love butterbeer and lattes, why not try this delicious latte-version? It's a great way to start the day.

Serving: 1

Total Time: 10 to 15 minutes

Ingredients:

- 2 tablespoons butter, unsalted
- 2 tablespoons light brown sugar, packed
- Whole milk, enough to fill a mug
- 1 teaspoon vanilla extract
- Dash ground cinnamon

Directions:

Step 1: Place the butter and sugar in a small saucepan. Set the saucepan on the stove over medium heat. Let the butter melt, while stirring constantly. Continue to cook until the sugar and butter and completely incorporated into one another.

Step 2: Stir in the milk, cinnamon and vanilla. Continue to stir until well combined.

Step 3: Keep cooking the mixture until it begins to boil. Once boiling, remove the pan from heat and carefully pour into a mug. Let cool for a minute or two before consuming.

Vegan Butterbeer

Vegans rejoice! You can enjoy butterbeer while still maintaining your vegan lifestyle.

Serving: 2

Total Time: 10 minutes

Ingredients:

- ½ tablespoon vegan butter
- ½ cup butterscotch syrup
- 1 cup vegan cream soda

Directions:

Step 1: Place the vegan butter and butterscotch syrup in a small saucepan. Set the pan on the stove over medium heat. Cook the mixture, while stirring, until the butter is melted and the mixture is bubbly.

Step 2: Remove the mixture from heat and let cool for a few minutes.

Step 3: Gradually pour the cream soda into the pan and stir until well mixed. The soda will fizz so be carefully to not let it overflow out of the pan as this will make a mess.

Step 4: Pour the butterbeer into 2 glasses and serve immediately.

Conclusion

Thank you again for downloading this book!

I wrote this book because I, like millions of other people, have a huge soft spot for Harry Potter. And I wanted to bring a bit of that magical world into our sometimes mundane lives. I hope you have found at least a few recipes in this book that sparked your interest.

Now the only left to do is to figure out which one of the delicious recipes you are going to try first!

If you found this book useful, please head over to Amazon and leave a review. It would be very much appreciated.

Click here to leave a review for this book on Amazon!

About the Author

Martha is a chef and a cookbook author. She has had a love of all things culinary since she was old enough to help in the kitchen, and hasn't wanted to leave the kitchen since. She was born and raised in Illinois, and grew up on a farm, where she acquired her love for fresh, delicious foods. She learned many of her culinary abilities from her mother; most importantly, the need to cook with fresh, homegrown ingredients if at all possible, and how to create an amazing recipe that everyone wants. This gave her the perfect way to share her skill with the world; writing cookbooks to spread the message that fresh, healthy food really can, and does, taste delicious. Now that she is a mother, it is more important than ever to make sure that healthy food is available to the next generation. She hopes to become a household name in cookbooks for her delicious recipes, and healthy outlook.

Martha is now living in California with her high school sweetheart, and now husband, John, as well as their infant daughter Isabel, and two dogs; Daisy and Sandy. She is a stay at home mom, who is very much looking forward to expanding their family in the next few years to give their daughter some siblings. She enjoys cooking with, and for, her family and friends, and is waiting impatiently for the day she can start cooking with her daughter.

For a complete list of my published books, please, visit my Author's Page...

https://www.amazon.com/author/martha-stephenson

Author's Afterthoughts

Thanks ever so much to each of my cherished readers for investing the time to read this book!

I know you could have picked from many other books but you chose this one. So a big thanks for downloading this book and reading all the way to the end.

If you enjoyed this book or received value from it, I'd like to ask you for a favor. Please take a few minutes to post an honest and heartfelt review on *Amazon.com*. Your support does make a difference and helps to benefit other people.

Thanks!

Martha Stephenson